Blue Throat Dancers

Poetry of Diaspora in Silicon Valley

Dr. Jyoti Bachani, Editor

Blue Throat Dancers

Poetry of Diaspora
in Silicon Valley
–Volume 5–

FIRST EDITION, January 2026
ISBN 978-1-965784-48-8 PAPERBACK
Printed in the United States of America, Canada, Australia,
Saudi Arabia, Japan, India, Brazil, and the European Union

Editor: Dr. Jyoti Bachani
Cover Graphic Design & Book Typography by Kurt Lovelace
Front cover by Arti Shishoo Verma, back cover by Jyoti Bachani
Cover type *Bauhaus Dessau* **Alfarn** by Céline Hurka,
Elia Preuss, Flavia Zimbardi,
Hidetaka Yamasaki, and Luca Pellegrini.
Editor name in **Jenson** by Robert Slimbach.
Back Cover names in **Gill Sans Nova**.
Titles and body text set in **Baskerville**.
Flourishes set in Emigre Foundry **Dalliance** by Frank Heine.
Emigre Foundry **ZeitGuys** by Bob Aufuldish, Eric Donelan.
Typefaces licensed Adobe, Linotype, Emigre, & URW GmbH.

PierianSpringsPress.Com
PIERIAN SPRINGS PRESS, INC
30 N GOULD ST, STE 25398
SHERIDAN, WYOMING 82801-6317

Foreword

This anthology is the fifth one by the poetry lovers who are part of an unpoetically named literary group called the Poetry of Diaspora in Silicon Valley. The community grew around me in the past decade as I hosted open-homes in my living room for multi-lingual poetry lovers. Five years ago Covid sent us to Zoom and from monthly meetings - we became a weekly Saturday night group of poetry-junkies. It helped us all make sense of the world together. As the new normal returns to the world, this anthology was a call to feel our way to our personal new normal. Best to read the call for poems that I sent to everyone to understand what I mean when I say we are feeling our way through the present.

Call for poems, sent to the community:

The anthology seeks poems that speak of the lived experience of the body, expressing our subtle essence, rich as a colorful tapestry woven from threads of sensations, smells, sounds, beliefs, values, memories and what we cherish and what we leave behind, every time we experience the dark isolation and silence that is part of the process metamorphosis. Consider the poems with:

Questions of identity with the courage to live and write as our unique, complex, non-dual selves in worlds defined by words and ideas that are always binary.

Personal change—of rupture, healing, and re-formation, with pleasure, pain and raw alchemy of evolution, beside the furious stillness of gestation.

Of rootedness and stability, commitment even as we adapt, to placate our muse, internal or external.

Of courage and failures, to share our stories and mythologies that give us ways to speak, dance, love, grieve, and always to carry on.

These are suggestions, not expectations. Send what feels real and true to you. Authentic, not performative is our ethos. We always welcome poems not related to the theme. Ambiguity, complexity, paradoxes, uncertainties and puzzles of not-knowing yet expressing with a certain clarity are some things that make poems interesting to me.

Why "Blue Throat Dancers"?

The title is tentative. I chose it because "dance" honors the movement of emotion through the body—the joy, the grief, the transformation we've each known through our engagement with poetry, with each other and the worlds we inhabit. The choreography of showing up, again and again, in our physical, feeling selves, for the poetry circle and blank pages (or screens) inviting us to write ourselves into being.

The blue throat comes from Hindu mythology. Shiva, the ascetic god, dancer of the cosmos—Natraj—is also known as Neelkanth, the blue-throated one. During the cosmic churning of the ocean for Amrit, the elixir of life, a deadly poison surfaced. Shiva drank it to save the world, holding it in his throat, so it would not harm him. His neck turned blue. We, too, in our bodies, carry things we cannot speak of. This anthology is a space to give words to that silent scream—to turn pain into poetry, to transmute the memory in ways to claim our truth. Shiva's other form is Ardhnarieshvar, half-woman-half-man, the non-binary existence. The holy water of Ganga Maiya would have drowned the world as it descended from the heavens to the earth, if Shiva had not volunteered his head of matted locks for it to land on. This is how we got life-affirming water in rivers that flow with all the music of bubbling mountain streams to the languid mergers with the call of the oceans, inspiring poets everywhere.

Why this Theme?

Because we've grown as we heard each other deeply. We've been changed, or as I like to say, each of us has "graduated". I see how many ripples have come from this circle, with each one of us becoming more confident in our voices to chart new paths. Creative work is solitary, yet I have this commitment from each of you who have shown up over the years to be in community with each other. There is value in this community that we each feel, even if we have only declared it by showing up, instead of words. Maybe because we have a streak of selfless service. I know we inspire and enable each other. I conceive this theme as both an anchor and a launchpad—a gift to ourselves of self-expressive craft and to our fellow poetry lovers and future readers as a glimpse into our journeys. This might be our final anthology.

On this day, June 10, 2025, the night of the Strawberry Full Moon—the world is witnessing several deep divisions: between the wealthy and the impoverished, the elite and the forgotten, the so called developed north and the global south, the old and the young, and fractures within families, divisions across languages, across borders and beliefs. In this churn, new possibilities are forming. What we've been holding in our throats—unspoken, unresolved, contained—can seed the fresh if we can be courageous enough to release it as poetry. The dance of Shiva reminds us that creation begins only after destruction. The elixir Amrit follows the poison. This anthology is closing the circle in respect of that same cosmic rhythm.

Three Invitations for Submission

1. Get Personal.

Share your story, as an autobiographical poem, a turning point, a dream, a scar, anything meaningful worthy of a poem. Written honestly, the personal becomes the bridge to the universal. Your journey—as an immigrant, a misfit, a seeker, a poetry-lover, a peacemaker, and a courageous warrior for love. What is the untold story that is written on your body?

2. Un-silence the Body.

Our bodies remember everything, the unsaid, the endured, the joy, the longing, the loving hand and the eye that saw, the cellular memory that persists, the sealed lips, the kiss, the dance coz hips don't lie. Let the poems speak of tensions and tenderness, of what we suppressed and what erupted as the body refused to be silenced. Perhaps expression will bring healing that is needed.

3. Write of the Metamorphosis.

The poetry circle has been an incubator. What emerged from it for you? What was lost in the process? What did you shed, and what remains? The caterpillar doesn't just grow wings—it dissolves first. Write about the destruction that made room for something new. Name what you're holding. Name what you've folded away. What dreams remain to keep you seeking?

Optional Writing Prompts

• What is subtle and mostly unseen in the world, that you sense deeply?

• What lyrics, chants, or songs are stitched into your emotional memory?

• Write about words that connected—or failed to connect—you to others.

• Where does your digital life bleed into the real? Or the other way around?

• What values are you holding onto like lifelines? What are you willing to let go?

• When did poetry intervene in your life? What did it heal, honor, or illuminate?

• How does your body store memory? What masks do you wear? When are you most authentic?

• What is ephemeral—and what deserves to be remembered?

A Note

Poetry connects us to see ourselves more clearly. It invites us to be brave, to own our past, hold our present and dream of a future we aspire for. Many of us have said "I am not a poet" and yet we kept showing up, for love of poetry, for ourselves, for each other, away from other demands of life and the world. Our vibrancy and energy come from this fearless, authentic, raw, open, and radically embodied presence, even when it was in a zoom room. The space we co-created was for us self-declared 'mis-fits' who somehow belonged, often with nothing in common, other than a desire to listen, by showing up with a gentle but quietly powerful presence, maybe with a poem or two, to share, with permission and more often, with an invitation, irshaad, or 'ek aur suntey jao'.

The Cover Art

I obviously chose to keep the tentative title as the real title, thanks to the terrific response in the form of submissions. A note about the cover art. The image on the front cover is by Arti Shishoo Verma, depicting the dancing feet of Shiva-Shakti, the Ardhnarieshawar (half-woman-half-man) form of Shiva, and the back cover is by yours truly, both cleaned up and arranged by our tireless publisher Kurt Lovelace. The radical openness with which I live and invite others into my world is how this work has emerged. In the spirit of cherishing this spirit of openness, I do not yet know how to decide whether this is the last of our anthologies or we will make more. What I have decided is that the name Poetry of Diaspora in Silicon Valley has to go. It has served its purpose of helping us coordinate our work using a Facebook-group. We are a solidly vibrant and connected community now. It has also become a phrase used by many others in the larger community around us. As we have been invited to perform at multicultural festivals, Diwali events in libraries and parks in cities of Cupertino, Sunnyvale and Belmont, with partnerships with poet laureates for poetry month events, with Mosaic America, Third Thursdays in Palo Alto and the longest standing one with India Currents, we have made multilingual poetry an essential part of the ecosystem around us. India Currents has launched a larger poetry community under the Poetry of Diaspora name. This is the best outcome that our group could have served: that poetry finds a place in the ordinary life of community. It is the time to dream fresh dreams, and our creativity must be used for creating a fresh vision and name now. Thank you to the readers - without whom we would remain silently in imagination. Read the poems, safely ignoring this commentary from an editor who is not qualified to edit other poets' poems.

Dr. Jyoti Bachani
California, September 2025

CONTENTS

Salma Arastu

Jyoti Bachani

Elham Malik

Prerona Mukerjee

Yogesh Patel

BLUE THROAT DANCERS

Salma Arastu

Salma Artsu is a Berkeley-based multidisciplinary artist creating harmony through painting, sculpture, calligraphy, and poetry. As a woman, artist, and mother, she explores the universality of humanity. With over 50 solo exhibitions worldwide, she has received several prestigious awards. Her poetry journey began with *Dard Ki Seedhiyan* (1980, Hindi), and her latest collection, *Seeking Oneness: Connecting Humanity, Soil and Soul*, was published in the UK in 2024.

१ ख़ुदा की रचना

इक इन्सान का ज़ुल्म दूजे इन्सान पर
देखके धरती काँप रही है
गिरा है बम धर्म के नाम पर कहीं
धर्म टूट रहा है
दो गज़ ज़मीं के लिए ये जंग
मौत थरथरा रही है
ख़ुदा की रचना
ये बंदे
एक सितमगर बनके बंदूक चला रहा है
दूजा भूखा नंगा तड़प रहा है
आज ख़ुदा अपनी रचना पर
ख़ुद ही शरमा गया है

२ रहम का दरिया

उसके हज़ारों हाथों से रहमत का प्याला छलकता है
पूरी कायनात पर
हर पल
बरसात बन कर बरसता है कभी
तो कभी प्यार बन कर दिलों को सींचता है
कभी हिदायत बन कर राह दिखाता है
तो कभी आश्वासन बन कर
हर दुखी इंसान को संवारता है
तुम भर लो दोनों हाथों से
इस प्रेम जल को हृदय में
और फिर बाँट दो उसके ही बन्दों में
पशु पक्षी और फूल पत्तों में
यही उसकी सीख है
यही इस जीवन का उद्देश्य
लुटाते चलो रहमान की ममता को
ये रहम का दरिया बहता रहे
उसके हाथों से रहमत का प्याला छलकता रहे
तो कहीं सूखा न कोई भूखा
न उदास रहे

३ प्रकृति का घूँघट

प्रकृति ने घूँघट ओढ़ लिया है आज
भीगी भीगी ओस की सफ़ेद चादर सी फैल गयी है चँहु ओर
ज़मीं से आसमां तक न लहरों के निशाँ है बाक़ी
न आसमाँ की रंगीनियाँ
आज प्रकृति ने घूँघट ओढ़ लिया है
भीगी भीगी'ओस का
पर कुछ पल उपरांत
सूरज पर जब यौवन छायेगा
तब उसकी चमकती प्यार भरी किरणे
सरका देंगी ये ओस का आँचल
निखर उठेगा कण कण
गुनगुनायेगी लहरें
जगमगायेगा सैन फ्रांसिस्को का शहर
ये ओस और सूरज का खेल
मैं अक्सर देखती हूं
और सोचती हूं
कि कितना ज़रूरी है कभी कभी
ओढ़ लेना एक चादर , डूब जाना अपने आप में
हटाए ये चादर फिर ज्ञान की किरणे
और ऊपर आ जाऊँ मैं सतह पर
हर रोज़ नयी नवेली बन कर

४ खूबसूरत पौधा

उसने दर्द को अपने अंदर सींचकर
एक खूबसूरत पौधा उगाया
रंग बिरंगे फूल लहलहा उठे
हरा भरा वातावरण मुस्करा उठा
दर्द पिघल कर अब
आँखों की कोरों से नहीं बहता
मन की आत्मा को सींचने लगा
सारी शक्ति, सारी प्रेरणा
उसने निचोड़ दी उसी पौधे में
उसकी खुशबू
उसका हरापन
उसकी शांत मधुर छाया
बाहर के लोगों को भी छांव देने लगी
कई मिलने वाले भी
सुगंधित पवन के झकोरे खाते
मुसकुराते आगे बढ़ते गए
वो भी मुस्करा उठी
और फिर सदियां गुज़र गयीं
अब भी अगर कभी दर्द बिलख कर
आँखों की कोरों से पिघल कर निकलता है
तो पूरी शक्ति से ढल देती है वो उसी पौधे में
देखो उसकी आँखे कितनी उज्ज्चल
और जीवन एक प्रेरणा

५ कविता

कविता की नहीं जाती
हृदय के कोने से उभरती है अचानक'
बहा ले आती है हर भाव को हर एहसास को
और शब्द बाँध लेते हैं उतने ही शब्दों को जितना बस में था उनके
और कविता लोट जाती है
कविता को तुम न समझोगे
वो इन शब्दों से गहरी , विशाल है
छायी है वो क्षितिज तक जीवन के
कुछ एक ये शब्दों की रचना
कविता की सम्पूर्णता नहीं
एक पल है
फैली हुई उस रचना का
जो वक़्त की सीमा से बाहर है

६ मेरा साया

मेरा साया मुझसे भी आगे चलते जा रहा है
में जितना तेज़ भागती हूं
वो उतना ही तेज़ भागता है
मेरा साया
मेरे नफ़्स का प्रतिबिम्ब
मेरे बस में नहीं और मेरे वजूद पर छाते जा रहा है
मन कहता है कि रुको
और पलट जाओ!
सूरज मेरे पीछे उठ रहा है
और में विपरीत दिशा में चल रही हूं
सूरज की रौशनी है हिदायत
सत्य और समर्थ
अगर मैं सूरज का सामना
करते हुए आगे बढ़ूंगी
बेधड़क बेझिझक
तो मेरा साया मेरे पीछे हो जाएगा
सूरज की किरणे मेरे कदमों के सामने
फैलती चली जायेंगी

७ सरकता वक़्त

अगर मोहब्बत के दरिया ने
न समेट लिया होता हमें
बिखर बिखर हो गए होते
हम किनारों के दामन में
यादों का दीपक जलाये रखना
ज़िंदगी के झरोखे पर
टिमटिमाती रौशनी में
चलते रहेंगे हम उम्र की राहों में
ये भी एक नियामत है
की भूल सकते है हम
वरना टूट कर बिखर जाते थे
हम यादों के तूफानों में
कुछ भीगे पल कुछ दर्द के मोती
चुने है हमने आज किनारों से
लहरें तो आकर चली गयी
सागर की सतहों में
उठाकर रखे हैं कुछ लिफाफे
कुछ खत और कुछ अशआर
शायद काम आये कभी
सरकते वक़्त की बाँहों में

८ प्रेम-प्रकृति का नियम

जी करता है सबको अपने
प्यार के आँचल में समेट लूँ
लुटाऊं वो मोहब्बत जो मिली है मुझे
मेरे रचयिता से
मुझे बनाने वाले दाता से
अठखेलियां करती है लहरें
जिस तरह किनारे से
हवाएं गुनगुनाती है संगीत
वृक्षों की डालियों को छूके
धरती बढ़ती आती है
आसमां को छूने
रात धुन में फिरती घूमती आती है
दिन को एक बार आलिंगन में भरने
प्रेम ही नियम है प्रकृति का
हर शै के वजूद का
फिर हम क्यों जुदा जुदा है
रूठे रूठे से खफा खफा है
आओ मैं भर लूँ
सबको अपने आँचल में

९ किनारों की खामोशी

लहरों क्यों टूट जाती हो बिखर जाती हो
किनारों का बदन छूते ही
क्यों अपना वजूद खो देती हो किनारों का बदन छूते ही
मैंने तुम में से हर एक को उमंग जोश के साथ
पूरी ताकत के साथ उमड़ते देखा है
तय करते देखा है कि
किनारों को बहा ले जाओगे तुम
वो हिम्मत देखी है वो उठान देखा है
में तो पूजती हूं तुम्हारी उस ताकत को
फिर क्या बात है
क्या बात है कि मुड़ के लौट जाती हो
किनारों का बदन छूते ही
किनारों को पाने की तमन्ना मेरी भी है
लेकिन गर यही अंजाम किनारे देते हैं तो मैं
बीच दरिया में जूझती उमड़ती उभरती
तुम में से हर उस लहर के पीछे आऊंगी
जो टूटी भी नहीं बिखरी भी नहीं
किनारो का बदन छूते ही
बोलो कोई है तुम में से ऐसी अछूती सी
जो ले चले मुझे अपने संग?
किनारों की खामोशी अब मुझे भाती नहीं

१० मुझे आज ना रोको

मैं सराबोर हूं
एक शक्ति से उस उमंग से
जो प्रेरित करती है
साधना के लिए रचना के लिए
मुझे रोको नहीं आज ना रोको
उड़ने दो उभरने दो आकाश में
मिट जाने दो सत्य को पाने के लिए
मेरी शक्ति विशाल है
तोड़ डालूंगी मैं झूठे बंधन
भींचे हुए जबड़े दर्द कर रहे हैं
विस्फोट को आने दो
फैलने दो , फैलने दो
इस पार से उस पार तक
नृत्य का जादू नहीं
संगीत की लय नहीं
ये तो गति है रफ़्तार है
जाने दो दूर तक
वहाँ - जहाँ वो एक हो सके
सम्पूर्णता के संग
उस बिंदु में जो शांत कर सके
भभकती ज्वाला को
आज रोको नहीं, मुझे आज ना रोको

११ आओ जूझ पड़ें हम मैदान में

आज हम सब दुखी हैं
उदास हैं
क्योंकि कोई हमारे पड़ोसियों को
ज़बरदस्ती घर से निकाल दे रहा है
उनकी पूँजी, उनकी मेहनत, उनका भविष्य
सब ख़त्म हो रहा है
हम दुखी हैं कि न सिर्फ हमारे पड़ोसी
हमारे भाई बहनों, हमारे चहेतों
हमारे परिवार वालों को भी कोई ज़बरदस्ती
घरों से निकाल के बम गिरा के
उनके घरों को जला दे रहा है
और बेचारे हमारे परिवार वाले
भूखे प्यासे भटक रहे हैं
अकेले रोते हुए,
मुर्दा बच्चों को गोद में लिए
ये कैसा वक़्त आ गया है कि
हम सिर्फ देख रहे हैं
हम सिर्फ सुन रहे हैं
रो रहे हैं, लेकिन कुछ कर नहीं पा रहे हैं
ऐसा क्यों है ?
आओ हम साथ हो जाएँ
और अपनी आवाज़ से अपने काम से
अपनी कोशिशों से

इस पापी सत्ता को ख़त्म कर सकें
परिवर्तन लाने वाला कोई हम में से ही तो है
गाँधी, नेल्सन हम में से ही तो हैं
वो कहानियां नहीं, वो गाथाएं नहीं हैं
वो सत्य की ताकत पर जूझने वाले इंसान ही तो थे
आओ सत्य की ताकत लेकर
हम भी झूज पड़ें मैदान में
अकेले अकेले दुखी रहने से मुश्किलें ख़त्म नहीं होती हैं

12. I Am Not Yet What I Want To Be

I am not yet there
Where I want to be.

The flying bird lowered her wings and asked me,
Where do you want to be?

Up in the sky like you, flying and free.
Come with me, she said,
Open your wings of imagination
And fly with me!

I am not yet what I want to be.

The waves responded instantly, gushing towards me,
What do you want to be?

A lover, a peacemaker, and connect all in nature and humanity.

They started rolling back saying,
Keep moving like us
And never stop
Until you become what you want to be,
Until you reach your grave.

But to constantly move and fly I need more energy.
How do I achieve that?

The wind passed by whispering,
Just surrender yourself to your creator.
Obey the laws of nature,
You will be blessed with more energy!

13. Let My Pen Speak The Truth

Let my canvas reveal the stories untold!

To pay attention,
And to be conscious is power.

But though we all are aware of genocide happening
In another part of the world,
Yet we are witnessing helplessly.

Thus, we all are accountable for this crime,
Because indirectly we are funding it too.

Holocaust is not forgotten yet—
Memories bring tears to the eyes,
And each soul shudders.

But still, we do not stop oppressing the Other?

There is no answer to that.

We are all children of Adam—
Greedy, selfish, and killers.
We are humans!

14. Solidarity

I can close my eyes.
I don't listen to the TV or radio,
Or watch the images on social media,
But my heart and soul are tremble
From the genocide happening
Right in the middle of the globe.

We can see it from all sides,
But we are quiet because it's the time of evil kings.
They are ruling the world, and we are helpless beings,
Perhaps afraid that one move from us
Might ignite a nuclear bomb
And end our world.

We don't want to end the world, we want to renew.
We want to regenerate the world.

So, let's gather to fight these evil kings—
Billions of people together can defeat
Two or three evil kings.

Yes, we need solidarity.
We must be compassionate and stand firmly
In solidarity with Gaza and all the oppressed.

Our little actions for the larger purpose
Are never in vain.

15. Find The Way Out

My body is hurting.
Blood is oozing out from scars
Given to me by enemies of humanity.

It is dark all around me,
As I don't see the end of this tunnel.

The present regimes around the globe—
Inhuman and greedy—
Are killing empathy, love, and compassion,
The sources of light and hope among humanity.

But I am lifting my body with each breath,
Crawling towards the end of the tunnel.

With my own heart's light,
I am paving through my path.

Join me, O humanity,
Igniting your own light for hope and justice
To reach the end of this darkness,
Crushing inhuman regimes and men greedy.

You all have the pilot of light within you—
Strike it with the fire of your sanity.

Fear has clouded your visibility;
Look deep in your heart to find the way out.

Jyoti Bachani

Dr. Jyoti Bachani is the founder of **Poetry of Diaspora in Silicon Valley**, a group of poetry lovers who meet regularly to read poems to each other. She is a strategy professor who professes that arts can humanize organizing. She has edited four poetry anthologies, guest edited the **Poetry for Organizing** special issue of the **Journal of Organizational Aesthetics** and translated over 200 poems from Hindi to English. She enjoys reading the poems by Vinod Kumar Shukla, Kunwar Narain, Sarveshwar Dayal Saxena, Ogden Nash, Hugh Prather, and many others. She enjoys listening to poems read out loud by passionate readers, in all languages.

For Kaavya (February 2025)

A lady fluent in silences
Sings poetry in languages
Buried in throats and books

With regal yearnings for

Ascetic Neelkanth's calm
With power to contain the poison
From the manthan in his throat
In the quest for Amrit

With the calm of oceans
To contain the restlessness of waves
Flowing freely from her eyes
With tides of unknowable sorrows

To find catharsis in unexpected delights
Of strangers opening doors
Taiko releasing nurses
Who dance by adjusting crutches

A guitar man banishes ignorance
With magnificent grace
Saying "I'll give you a key"
Commanding "just play"

Singing to invite us to
Discover our mojo
Arranging our fears in a
Ring of fire
Around the Natraj
To remind us of the eternal Tandav

The moment Uni-verse manifests

Being Love I (October 2020)

If you are with me
I love you
Like I loved my mother
Who raised me
Providing food, clothing and shelter
So my body survived

If you are not with me
I love you too
Like I loved my father
Who abandoned me
Leaving hope, stories and dreams
So my spirit thrived

Loving is my nature
Of that fate I am certain

Self-doubt plagues its' expression
For I am intimately familiar
With my body's hunger
And my spirit's fantasies
Neither of them
Being permanent

The self-doubt and self-assured confidence
Ebb and flow, as is the nature
Of all that I surrender to

The sunrise and the sunset
The waxing and waning of the moon
The birth and death of all that is cherished,
Mothers, fathers, flowers and birds that fly
A bit like spirits
Leaving only the faint memory
Of a shared breath
Or a sigh.

Being Love 2 (October 2020)

He does his best to endure my words
With stoic unresponse
I suffer his silence with equal patience
Expressing my unwavering affection

Our love is eternal
Locked in a centuries old dance
Knowing it is only safe
In its unrequited state

We both wait for time to pass
Surrendering to the inevitable change of seasons

Love, Us, Nature, Words, Silence,
Each flowing with their own
Unreasonable reasons.

Being Love 3 (October 2020)

You have a rain check for
Hugs to claim whenever you wish

I am aware that this evokes disgust
I wish I deserved it but it is unearned, Yet
I accept it for that is where we are now

Its the very same disgust I feel too
Albeit for things with no name, no shame and
No words, despite my prodigious outpourings

I am adept at hearing your silence
I am aware I don't comprehend your verse
I am rushing into projects I am unqualified for
I am pouring out words that are utter nonsense

I am becoming the one expressing all that is disgusting
Releasing what was once upon a time forcibly poured into me

I am reclaiming my old body by cleansing
By passing forward the burdens it was carrying
My broken body is transferring its cargo safely
Into a vessel large and empty enough to contain it
Shoulders and spine strong enough to bear its' weight
Heart and hands tender enough to bury its sharp edge

With a faint hope that someday

I'll caress a head in my lap
When its ready to pour the tears out
After the poems too are exhausted
For coding it for the eternity it came from
To be reunited with it, in beauty.

The Presence (Oct 2020)

It was short
It was quick
Yet it was epic

It was real
It was imagined
You see it was on Zoom

It was naughty
It was playful
It was unexpected

It was expressive
It was literary
Yeah it was exquisite

It was sincere
It was earnest
From the start it was hopeless

It was fragrant
It was transparent

They mastered how to transcend
They were totally innocent

It was true
It was false
Seen as a duel, it was
A silently sung duet

It was love
It was passion
Masquerading as
Supreme indifference

It was courage
It was trust
Nah! It was all bogus

It was ephemeral
It was eternal
It made time stand still

It was colorful
It was brittle
Old dried flower
Pressed in a book

It was a curse
It was a prayer
The answer to all questions

It was immersive
It was evocative
Past, present & future

It was kind
It was cruel
Demanding total surrender

It was together
It was separate
Baited breath all air

It was public
It was private
So Godamm intimate

It was beautiful
It was flawed
It was kingtsugi art

It was expansive
It was contained
The unending dance
Of a DNA strand

It was dark
It was light
Hard to tell
Dawn or dusk

It was tenacious
It was tender
A web of gossamer

It was smiles
It was cries
Newborn tiny miracles

It was visible
It was hidden
One wave of an endless ocean

It was joyful
It was sad
A hundred percent natural
Not unlike an itch scratched

It was petulant
It was wisdom
The comment
"Emperor's naked"

It was a fairytale
It was once upon a time
Yup to be remembered and retold
By all for all times

It was stagnant
It was ever-flowing
Deep glacier pristine territory

It was hot
It was cold
Ice burn thawing
A frozen bruise

It was searing
It was soothing
Unbearable, like an addiction

It was worthless
It was precious
A child's paperboat

It was a fragile egg
Safe in a nest
Now a bird taking flight
The nest left behind.

Feeling Love

I was the fearless one
Till I met the one fluent in silence

He wouldn't give me his poem
And insisted I will always be a tree

I was a tree wannabe

Till I met the one who could see
The woman in me

Filling me with fear
For more injuries than I could bear
He saw that So was clever
To disguise himself to get near

Bridging the distance through a distant one
Who knew how to go away and yet belong
New ways of being enabled by technology
That I insisted on seeing as a mere film.

Even as I pined for Jasmine, I surrendered
To the seduction of lavender

A sparkling veil to hide my fear
Reassurances traded with the messenger
"I am alright" as he told me
"Don't hide"

I accepted
It is good to be alive

To celebrate this sensitive body
Kept safe in a caged state
Trusting him with the keys, saying
"you release me" and so beautifully.

He didn't want
The key or the responsibility
For it really belonged
To our invisible friend

The one who haunts us both
A guardian angel to one
A ghost to the other

We both surrender, asunder
Like all epic lovers

Except

Our warring families weren't in conflict
With each other, but within themselves
Passing their violent legacies to us

The show goes on
Sad stories are popular and sell well.

Who cares of private joys
Of the youthful ambition
That is inevitably sacrificed
For its strong and too driven

No one except the very old
Obsess about such a memory
Everyone else preaches Moving on.

The modern love song says
Breakup, wear makeup
There is Tinder

Empowered woman can make
The first move boldly
No mumble, just Bumble

Act on impulse.
No room for feelings,
In a hurried world.

Pregnant Pause (October 2020)

He takes pride in what he creates
She in what she nurtures

Creativity itself.

He thinks its up to isolation and genius
She is convinced no man is an island

Searching, being left behind
Knitting, rebuilding her tribe

To soothe her crying child
With make-believe play
Of collective dreams from
The single ray of hope
That everyone holds on to

As time marches on
Reminding all of their
Bloodied pasts, fearful futures
Insisting on the moment
To be pushed pulled apart
In its all too brief
Pregnant pause.

Ode to Love (October 2020)

Hugs are negotiable
Love is not – it just is.

Afraid of it's power
He runs from it
She turns to it.

Their conflict is over this four letter word
Obvious to all but unclear to the muddled souls.

He admits he is a lover of hugs
She confesses to being hypersensitive to touch.

Always careful to ask "Would you like a hug?"
When comforting others

Self-effacing her feelings
Self expression in-check
Socialized as a girl-child

Acting out their assigned roles
Helpless, both feel the burn
Periodically reassuring each other
"Relax" "All is well" "Take good care"

This is their evolution, a trip of
Isolation, connection, separation
Emergence to what is yet to be

Patience as their friend
Endurance as their means
Perseverance as their state
They learn to surrender
To the great unknown
In service and devotion
To the unending ode to love.

In-Betweenness

On meeting rejection
I was seduced into
Self-defense
In the name of love

I am open they are closed
I was tempted to explain

I am capable of knowing pain
Without being attached to containing it
Complaints or crying simply rearrange or spread it
With our collective delusion that we let it go

We, instead, drive it underground
Deeper into our heart

My mother earth has a molten hot core
She keeps contained under her green blanket
Of forest and lush oceans of everflowing love

It spews out through mountain peaks
To join the clouds
As Vesuvius or other names
Covering all in ashes as it falls back
To let us know Mama's had enough

But do we stop?

Silence or words both are traps
For that which is pure ehsaas (Hindi for sensed)

That in-betweenness is where I dwell

Between a rock and a hard place
Between a lake and the Pacific bay
Between sleep and awake
Between night and day
Between yours and mine
Between open and close
Between friend and foe
Between pain and pleasure
Between now and forever
Between letting go and holding on

Honoring my being
For this precious expression
Give but for a moment
I get to be a part of eternity
I am forever in motion
I am now resting in peace

Whatever it is, it will be
Come or go, choose or surrender
Reject or Revere, pause or go
Cherish if you can
And its just as well
If you won't.

Feminine Spaces (21 September, 2021)

'It wasn't easy' spoken in soft tones
only to a trusted old friend
who witnessed the unfolding of your life
from the safe distance of another continent
a culture you left behind as an immigrant
for its oppression towards girls and women.

Words as a euphemism or a gross understatement
Screaming out loud with profanities galore
might better suggest this kind of pain
beyond the imagination
that inhabits the body
mind and spirit
in ways that brings a profound calm
of a detached life
where each breath
is the last gasp
before the momentary respite
longing for relief
of death, that too laughs.

Moitreyee Chowdhury

Moitreyee is a psychotherapist and artist. She is passionate about building a community, that recognizes the beauty of diversity and works towards equity. Moitreyee enjoys meeting friends from across the globe, learning new languages, art, poetry, and wandering amongst tall trees. She seeks to understand the amalgamation of science, literature, arts, nature, and its relationship with the world.

Birth. Silence.

Birth, body, hold, walk, sleep, run, jump
Sing, dance, cry, scream.
Music.
And tunes go out.
Colors. Blackout.
Run run run
Stay. Hold hold.
Scream. Scream. No noise.
Sound from the sky.
All silent.
Run, wait. Silence.
Birth. Wait. Next.

The Whisper and the Sun

A whisper becoming loud.
I looked around. The wind was speaking. I heard the whisper
    again. Was it the rustling trees.
Lost, I kept going on, the whisper walking with me.

The air is still. Becoming difficult to breathe.
The trees knew and waved their branches. I
Looked up, smiling in gratitude. Silent companions.

I have come far. Resting with my whisper, I looked around.
    Whisper told me it was time. I smiled knowingly. The mountain
    right there. Sun rises behind it.

Sun doing what it does. Burning, shining, lightening the world.
    I smiled at the Sun. Reaching out. I will be the Sun.
    Whisper smiled. It was waiting for me.

Saswati Das

Saswati Das, an engineer by profession and a poetess by heart, lives in Milpitas, California, and writes poems and fiction in both English and Hindi. She had published a poetry book in English, **Fragrant Flute of Fire**, and another in Hindi named **Kalpanain**. Recently, some of her Hindi poems have also been in the *Poetry of Diaspora in Silicon Valley* group's anthology, **A Memory Book of Poetry of Diaspora in Silicon Valley**.

उधार की हँसी

क्या मुझको तुम उधार दोगे
तुम्हारी थोड़ी सी हंसी?
खुश्क सालों का मौसम था वह,
बारिश न हुई थी कितने साल!
तपती धूप में मेरी रूह
तिश्नगी से थी बेहाल!

"चंद लम्हों की उल्फत का"
दिया था मैंने इश्तिहार,
ख्वाहिशों के जमघट में
न मिला था मुझे कहीं करार!

दर्द के कुछ व्यापारियों से
हुई थी मेरी गुफ्तगू,
उनके दिल में भी थी
चंद खुशियों की आरजू!

उन्हीं के संग मैंने रहाइश-गाह बसाया,
किया खुद पे एतबार;
शिरकत में पाई इफादियत अपनी,
न मांगा किसी से फिर उधार!

A Little Bit Of Laughter

translation of उधार की हँसी

Will you please lend me a little bit of your laughter?
Dry, dry was the season there
Not a single drop of rain,
In the scorching heat, my soul wandered
In the search of water, insane!

A few moments of love
I had asked for in the site;
In the crowd of desires
My heart found no respite!

In the caravan, I met
Some merchants of pain;
They too had pining for
A few drops of rain!

With them I build
My abode of love;
Trusted myself again
In the communion I found my worth
I was never ever the same!

एक ख़याल

एक ख़याल जो कभी
उतरा था मेरे आँगन में;
हवा जिसे उड़ाके ले गयी थी
किसी अनजान गली में!

उसे ढूँढती हूँ में
हर शहर हर नगर
की शायद वो मिल जाए!

वह ख़याल जो
एक नगमा बन सकता था;
या फिर बन सकता था कोई तरन्नुम !

वह ख़याल जो
दिलो को बदल सकता था;
ला सकता था अमन
रंजिशों में!

रोशनी फैला सकता था
बंद कमरों में!

वह तसब्बुर
जो गा सकती थी
वसल की ग़ज़ल
जुदाई के रसम में !

वह ख़याल जो किसी को
आया ही नही!
वह शायद आज भी पड़ा होगा लावारिस,
किसी बेरुख़ी डगर में !

सिकुर के बैठा होगा
जाड़े की शाम में
एक नये ज़हन
की गर्मी की आस में!

या फिर निशब्द शिथिल
पड़ा होगा
बेदिल बर्फ़ीली वादियों में !

अगर तुम्हे वह ख़याल
मिल जाए कभी
किसी भूली बिसरी राह में
तो कहना उसे
की मैं कल रात भी बेदार थी
उसकी बाट जोहते
अपनी अधूरी नज़्म लेके !

Thought

translation of एक ख़याल

A thought that had alighted upon my garden
Wind blew which away to an unknown land..
I quest for it
In every city, in every town
In the hope to find it some day!

A thought that could have been a verse of love
Or could have been a melody!
A thought that could have changed hearts.
Could have brought peace in enmity!
Could have shone light in the closed dark rooms !

An imagination that could have sung the music of union
In the season of separation!
An idea that occurred to none !

The thought might still be lying orphaned
In some apathetic roadside,
Shivering in a cold winter evening
Waiting for the warmth of a mind!

Or perhaps it might be lying silent
In the hopeless frozen mountains!

If you find that thought one day,
In some lost aimless lane
Tell it that I have been awake for it
Even last night
With my unfinished poetry!

जहर

मुझे बेइन्तहा मोहब्बत हैं
उस जहर से,
जो मुझे तिल-तिल कर मारती हैं|

वह जहर कोई नशा नहीं,
ना ही हैं कोई जुनून!

वह पावन हैं एक शिशु की मुस्कान की तरह,
वह शीतल हैं हवा के झोंके की तरह,
वह मेरा अस्तित्व हैं,
वह हैं मेरा सुकून|

मृत्यु मेरे सामने था
मैं खुद को रोक ना पाई,
ज़िन्दगी मुझे बुला रही थी
वह मुझको टोक न पाई;
चंद लम्हों की बात थी,
मैंने किया नहीं था गौर
मेरे निगाहों के सामने तक़दीर मेरी
ले ली थी वह मोड़|

आज शिकायत नहीं हैं अपनी रूह से,
ना ही राहों का हैं डर,
एक सिद्धांत लिया था मैंने उन गलियों में
आज वही हैं मेरा मुकद्दर|

Poison

translation of जहर

I am in insatiable love with a poison
That kills me inch by inch.

The poison is not an infatuation
Nor is it an obsession;

It's pure like the smile of a child
It sedates me like a breeze of air,
It's the essence of me
It is the peace of my prayer!

Death was in front of me,
It asked for my embrace.
Life was calling me
It could not abate my pace!

It was the call of the moment
I took the stride;
In front of my eyes, my fate
Took the turn of life.

I have no complaints with my soul
Perhaps it was an epiphany;
I made a choice in those lanes
Today that is my destiny.

गुमनाम गली

बचपन की उस गुमनाम गली का
आज एक नाम है
बचपन की उस अनजान गली की
आज एक पहचान है !

गली के दो पहलुओं में
हुआ करती थी
कुछ रीढ़हीन झाड़ियाँ
वह दब गई हैं आज
बड़ी बड़ी क्रिस्टलीय इमारतों के नीचे !

त्रिकोण , चौकोन, षटकोण!
इन मुकम्मल आकारों के नुकीले कोने
चुभते हैं मेरी रूह को !

गली के मोड़ पर हुआ करता था
मनोज चाचा का दुकान
आज उसका निशान तक नहीं हैं !
मनोज चाचा भी गुम हो गए हैं कहीं
अनगिनत बेनाम चेहरों की भीड़ में !

उन आब-दार इमारतों में
दो इमारतों के बीच
है एक छोटी सी उच्छृंखल पग-डंडी !
जहा कभी धुप नहीं पहुँचती !
ऐसा लगता है जैसे किसी ने
उसके हिस्से का सूरज छीन लिया हो !

इमारतों के अंदर चंद कागज के फूल
दिलाते हैं झूठी आस
एक नयी सुबह की !

बाहर कुछ बेजुबान यात्रियों का काफिला
हर रोज़ तै करता है सफर
अँधेरी गली से अँधेरे बक्सों तक !

Yearning For Amorphous Beauty

translation of गुमनाम गली

Down the streets of my childhood
As I walk alone -
I find no horizon!

My panoramic view blocked by
Homogeneous crystalline structures –
Rectangles, Triangles, Hexagons!

Shapes perfect and symmetrical
Left no margin for errors!
The sharp corners prick my conscience!

Inside,
There is a paradise
Untimed Cool breeze
Paper flowers
Milky Rain!

Little children can't look outside
They have no windows!
Caged in mirrors
That reflected one another with no distortion!

Outside,
The scorching heat dried up the soul!
Humans reduced to breathing zombies!
Marched towards the abyss!
Apathetic mountains count the stars
Endangered free birds yearn for the amorphous beauty!

तफ़तीश

यह गोलियों की आवाज़,
शोर यह अजीब;
यह जननी के अश्रु,
तिफ्ल की चीख!

यह तन्हाई का आलम,
अमीरों की भीख;
यह गुमराह नस्लें,
नशे में मुंह मीक!

वो शिकस्त निगाहें,
वह शुष्क गुल;
वह अधूरी तालीम,
वह डूबा उसूल!

वह अपाहिज़ सी ज़िंदगी,
बिन आवाज़ के संगीत;
पूछती है हमसे,
आज की तारीख-

जो कहा, सुना, किया,
क्या वह सही था?

Conundrum Of The Conscience

translation of तफ़तीश

The sound of the guns
Reverberating cries;
Tears of the mother
Corpse of the child!

Realm of scarcity
Apathy of the rich;
Youths going astray
Soaked in seas!

Those looks of fear
Flowers smelling foul;
The half sunshine
The numbed soul!

Incapacitated lives
Singing voiceless song
Ask us today
In a gloomy dawn!

What we said, heard, did;
Were those right?

Shruti Dixit

Shruti is excited to share her poetry with the world. In writing poetry she experiences magic. For words, lines, whole rhymes flow —not from her but through her. They help her recognize light and she finds herself going back to these poems for herself—in sharing these, she hopes you will find peace and joy—and that they will bring a chuckle. In other life stuff, she's surrounded by an amazing family and the best of friends; and loves nature. This love finds expression as a landscape architect, and as a teacher of architectural and landscape design.

On Light And Dark

My thoughts–they are like butterflies.
One on one tree here getting my attention,
And before I know it, the color is better,
And they go flitting in another direction.
What was it that I was thinking a minute ago?
What was it that seemed overpowering but
    something else has taken over now?

Something dark comes along sometimes.
They are scary thoughts but out of curiosity I go deeper.
It seems the pull of darkness is stronger than that of light.
And then I realize that darkness has a need to pull.

Light has no need to fight, to pull, to search, to do anything.
Light is just always there.
Even knowing, I tend to forget.
The darkness tries to take hold–a whirlwind
    of worries, of negativity, of fear beckons.

And then sometimes it's as if magic happens,
Light gives a little nudge.
It rolls its eyes and asks me to wake up.
It asks me why I waste my time,
Thinking up worries that may never strike.
And I find myself smiling- Light has won.

For this moment.

Playmate

I was coming to meet you,
And saw you from a distance.
Then I heard you.
You were calling…
Consistently.
Insistently.
I almost ran,
Impatiently waited.
As the traffic signals held me back.

And then we met.

You came running to greet me.
I met you smiling and playfully kicked.
You called me,
Come a little further ahead.
Come on–you gently nudged me.
Your sounds became louder.
They surrounded me.
All I could think of was you
And how beautiful this play felt to me.
I smiled as I splashed,
Creating waves of my own.
I couldn't seem to have enough
Of hearing you crash upon the shore.

First one, then another.
So many ripples.
They felt like sisters and brothers
Out in the sun.
All my own.
Taking away from me,
What I don't need.
Healing me,
In ways unknown and unseen.
Leaving behind a piece of itself,
As joy in my heart.
As song in my head.
Thank you to my playmate this afternoon.
You have left me beaming,
And I wish you well.

NOW

The wind is calling,
It says hello.
The clouds show up,
In forms galore.
They move,
They dance,
They whirl around.
Every minute, every second.
There is a new now.
I stare in wonder.
And I smile.
As my breath,
And the wind and the universe entwine.

You Are Always Free

You are always free.
It is your thoughts which keep you chained,
In a world of right and wrong.
In a world of should and musts.
In a world where no matter what,
As long as possible the show must go on.
Until you reach a point in time,
When you are called to step off the grind.
Maybe it's the body that forces you to rest
To sit for a moment and then reflect.
What have you been busy with?
Where are you off to when there's nowhere to get.
Maybe if we loosen the grip,
Of those thoughts which keep us enmeshed,
Very soon we begin to realize,
We are quite free
Always in flight.
It's a moment of delight,
When this we begin to realize.

Waiting

I have been waiting for the words to come to me.
Silently,
Patiently,
Like they used to.
I would be cleaning the dishes,
And an entire poem would find itself penned down.
In a matter of minutes, if not seconds.
I wrote the words, but they had come to me.
And then I got busy.
The noise of life took over.
And though the words may have been knocking,
I could not hear them.
Over time I realized–
I missed my play.
I missed the words.
Many months passed like this.
Me in waiting,
And the words and rhymes probably knocking.
Until one day,
Of its own accord,
The heart gently nudged.
It's time—it said.
For what–I wondered as I paused.
To stop waiting.
If you are looking for words,
And enjoy dancing with them,
Like any relationship,
You need to give it time.

You need to make space.
You need to go past the noise.
So, this morning with my cup of tea,
That is exactly what I did.
And lo and behold!
Not only are the words coming.
In their own unique and usual way,
The thoughts they transmit,
Are guidance.
Which goes beyond me and my noise and my limited ways.
I pause as I recognize–
Incredible Grace.
And the only thing I can do,
Is to surrender to these words and to smile in gratitude.
What I was waiting for was already always there.
And though I write about words today,
I see all of life at and in this play!

On Identity

Very often we define
Our life based on our sense of Identity.
Before we can even realize,
In a subtle sneaky way,
That identity becomes a prison.
It is so one dimensional.
That identity becomes a wall
Preventing us from seeing our all.

Whether it is trying to be an ideal,
Defining for yourself a Ram like identity.
Or working hard at a corporate job,
Or staying at home being a mom.
There are moulds the universe seems to have carved;
Sometimes defined by choice,
Or sometimes by what we call fate.
Sometimes we try to create a version
    of who we thought we should be.
The 'Should' itself of course being limited,
Defined by us through society.

There comes a point when we need to break free.
To not be defined by identity.
And not limit oneself
Based on what society or what we think we should be.

Ram can be a stay-at-home mom.
Sita can do a corporate job.
The children can run the show,
Or maybe we can all just be playing in the snow.

Let yourself be.
In the moment, of the moment, for the moment.
Not be chained by the shackles of identity.
Embracing rather what is waiting for thee.
The Whole Universe is yours.
THAT is your identity ;)
The funny thing is...
It has no identity.

:)

Anuradha Gajaraj-Lopez

Anuradha holds a postgraduate degree in Journalism and Mass Communication. She was a reporter with The Times of India and later a Special Correspondent with The Asian Age national newspaper in India. Anuradha has authored over 20 books, the most popular among them being the "Agasthiyar Vazhipaadu' series. Her books are sold in countries across the world including UK, US, Canada, Australia, Italy, India, Germany, France, Mexico, Japan, Thailand, Malaysia, Mauritius and other countries. She lives with her family in Clovis, California.

Agasthiyar Vazhipaadu
https://www.amazon.com/author/anuradhagajaraj-lopez

Agasthiyar Vazhipaadu (agastyagnanapeetamca.blogspot.com)
https://agastyagnanapeetamca.blogspot.com/

Agathiyar Valipaad - YouTube
https://www.youtube.com/channel/
UCEons12UnOcSwSf2XUfxzRw

Shiva & Ganga

Unleashed she descended
With all the fury of the force divine
Threatening, to destroy, destroy all in her way
All obstacles were but wisps of straw in her sway
As she danced her cosmic dance away

He looked up with a calm smile on his lips
With arms resting lightly on his skin covered hips
And gently caught her fury in his matted locks
Absorbing, absorbing all her force softly within

For He alone, the Absolute matched her in every way
For He alone, had the power to withstand her divine play
And so, He responded to her strong inner call
And then let her flow calmly and serenely on
She-Ganga, the sustainer of all life!

Ardhanareeshwara

In just one fluid movement he strove
To draw her into his body own
Bestowing half of himself
And accepting her half
Though,
Strange it seemed -
A body half man-half woman
The body of Aradhanareeshwara

The mingling of two forces
But not perfect halves to
Make one complete whole
For, not perfection they sought
Nor completeness
But a harmony of their own
Of the Aradhanareeshwara

In the seven sacred steps
Of matrimonial rites,
In the making of the conjugal bliss
They -
The human male and female sought
This harmony as revealed
In the sacred form of Aradhanareeshwara

Representing an analogy
That many an ancient temple told
In poetry of stone that every
Shiva lingam showed
The symbolical form of the Aradhanareeshwara
The bliss that the creator found
When the atman reached its home
Or the kundalini shakti sought
As she inched her way to her Lord
The physical manifestation as
Seen in the Aradhanareeshwara

And so, the human couple, it seems
Hold the balance in creation
As together they reach the harmony found
In the mingling of body, mind, and soul
As none can, but only they can do
And create peace, love and
Harmony untold
In this the creation of
The Aradhanareeshwara

When Shiva Wept

Shoulders powerful raised her body inert
As feet thundered a deadly rhythm
Cymbals clashed and trumpets wailed
In time to his terrible dance

Mother Earth quaked
Rivers rose in spate
And mountains fell
Adding time to his terrible grief

She fell in parts, his own Sati
She who had been part of his dance divine
Now she lay
Scattered over terrain
As Shiva wept and danced his terrible dance

For even He - the Absolute
Prime of the Triumvirate
Was not free from the decree of fate!

The Secret of Chidambaram

What is the secret of chidambaram"
I asked with curiosity

"Look," said Shiva
And opened the curtains
"What is there? Nothing!",
I said in surprise

"Isn't that the very
Source of this world ?",
Said Shiva laughing!

Nataraja

Jumping into my heart like lightning
Danced Thai, Thai,
The Nataraja of Chidambaram !

Coming like a breeze
Removing the veil of illusion
He blessed me, that Maheshwaran!

"Om Namaha Shivaaya, Shivaaya, Shivaaya namaha
Chant this sacred mantra 108 times daily
And climb the stairs of Kailasa
My dear children,
So saying he blessed
Salutations! Salutations! Salutations to him!

God-Self

What is God?
But the self expressing itself!
The self experiencing itself!
And In that moment of untold bliss
The self discovering itself!

Appa's Blessed Feet

From the depths of sorrow
Grows the deepest devotion
In the grief you feel
Flowers the bliss of non-attachment
As you let go of human bonds
One by one
And clasp tightly
Our father's blessed feet!

Tears you shed, over a future
Once you dreamt and lost
From those dried tendrils
Will the fire of knowledge bloom
Every little scene of this illusion lost
Soon replaced with his light
Of eternal peace
Hold on to our father's blessed feet!

Know that what you grieved for
Was just an illusion
As you hear his gentle and sweet
Response to your prayers
You have awakened
O my sleeping soul
As your hands touch his dear blessed feet!

What joy! What joy!
The angels dance and sing
One more sister is now fully awake!
She us free from the chains of illusion
She is free to soar, the angels sing
As they too swirl around his blessed feet!

Do you feel his tender hands
Your shoulders touch?
As he lifts you up
And walks you on his path
The path of light
That dispels all darkness?
That path made holy by his blessed feet!

O Yogi!

Who is the teacher?
Who, the one who learns?
Know this,
It is the self seeking itself
In this game of illusion
It has deigned to play!

There truly is
No beginning, No end!
All that is experienced
All that is expressed
All that is in between
Exists neither here nor there!

Why seek elsewhere?
that which is already known
In that self of the self
Is truly not else
But Only light, O Yogi!

Sanyasi

Saffron clothes do not a renunciate make
Not on mountains, or deep forest
Can he be found!

Look around,
He that in worldly duties seemingly intent
Holds no anger, desire or lust within

He, the true renunciate
Having the six traits renounced
Action performs,
In God alone his whole being immersed!
Of the world, in the world, he may yet be
Yet, he is the true Sanyasi!

Siddha

Not by his piety
Nor knowledge
Not as man or god
Nor even by siddhis
May he be known!

He, is a Siddha
Wisdom personified
Beyond all limitations
Of this,
The created world!

He the conqueror
Mind and ego
the great enemies
Of this
The manifested world!

Beyond all dualities
Untouched is he
By wrath, lust
Or other little human
frailties!

Not even bound,
by duty Is he-
He,
the 'perfected' being!

The Siddha! Perfect!
He the epitome of
the perfected being
As The absolute Meant
all of us to be!

Sanyasi

Matted hair, calloused feet,
Tattered clothes he wears
Eating rotten food with relish
A mangy cur at his side, he rests

"Who is he? This beggar in rags
What an eyesore," the priest exclaimed
Grabbing a stick, he strode forward
"Away, you filthy animal," he yelled!

Letting out a hearty laugh
The filthy man stood tall
"Pray, what is filth? what is clean?
Nary a difference I see," he calmly said

He clapped his hands,
"This world you see,
feel and hear
Lo! Look! It is all gone!" He said

T'was but an instant,
As the priest stood aghast
In a blinding flash,
The entire world disappeared!

Fell he to the ground
Clasping firmly the feet
The Avaduta's blessed frame
Begger then, now, the very Guru he revered !

What is God?

What is God?
But the self expressing itself!
The self expressing itself!
And the self discovering its self
In the moment of untold bliss!

Reena Kapoor

Techie turned writer, playwright and photographer, Reena Kapoor grew up all over India as an "army brat". That wandering sensibility is reflected in her debut poetry collection ARRIVALS & DEPARTURES: JOURNEYS IN POEMS

Reena's poetry and stories have appeared in *Bluebird Word*, *433 Magazine*, *Literary Yard*, *Discretionary Love*, *Flash Fiction Forum*, *Ariel Chart*, *Tiny Seed Journal*, *Writing in a Woman's Voice*, and *India Currents*. Four plays by Reena were produced by *EnActe Arts* in 2021; and her latest full length play was selected for *EnActe's* **New Works Festival** in 2023.

Reena's been a **Citizen Historian** with **The 1947 Partition Archive** collecting oral histories from witnesses of India's Partition since 2011.

She graduated with an undergraduate engineering degree from **IIT Delhi** and a Master's from **Northwestern University**. She can be found at **ArrivalsAndDepartures.SubStack.Com**

My Mother And I In A Photograph

[A grief-love poem in 3 Tankas]

My mother, and I,
fill a photo holding hands
weeks before she's void.
Still see her hands, venous, dry,
lined with scripts I fail to read.

Her body weighted
with childhood trauma; shrunk, bent,
ill. Her purpose lost,
scattered in ashes of one
who loved her so completely.

Willfully blind, I
sit holding her. Restive, not
heeding asteroids
headed for this merry earth—
frothy bubble that's my world.

I Got In A Quarrel With Time

I quarreled again
with time, today,
that strident fool!
I tire of his hubris,
his silly ridicule,
When I run out,
what will you do?

He's fully convinced
life travels one way.
The losses mount,
dusted when I'm done.
The end renders you
pauper as you were
a naked newborn!

That's where you're wrong,
dear time, I retort,
Life's no rigid arrow,
nor a one lane way,
nor a planet's pull,
nor a written fate.
So my questions ensue…

How will you repeal days
I've already lived?
love I've been given,
love I've given away?
How will you make me
unsee, unfeel, untaste,
unhear, or un-inhale?

If it's lived it's sealed,
embossed, engraved,
in indelible scripts,
'neath your shifting sands.
Our brimming pasts
lock treasures in
chests veiled from theft.

So, threaten all you want.
But do come by
for my casual display
of the things I keep
to show our gods
what I constructed
my immortalities from!

"You're Out"

I don't forget those
games we played.
Serious endeavors
told us all we needed

to know about who
was friend or foe.
Someone who lied
if you weren't looking.

Someone who refused
a close call not in
their favor or took one
extra, not really theirs.

I touched your shirt,
you didn't feel it...
the touched ones
insist it wasn't so.

Who's to say
who was right?
Yet our certainty
made us sure

we knew friends
from enemies who
we declared were those
cheaters, cheaters, pumpkin-eaters!

Years later we met them
and wow, fine they were,
fine people! Our certainty
met a stupid death

despite our memories'
claim they never lied
about "the facts"!
I wonder now how

many of today's
certainties will wither
tomorrow in a
stupider hubris

as we'll find them,
those "others" are
human too; hardly
what we made them
out to be. Instead,

like me they try
to play along
clumsily by this life-
game's ambiguous rules.

Crawl Space Creatures

Is that mice or rats in my basement?
—no difference to this tale really
for one day, began this horrid squeaking
I called in the man to get rid of it all
He proposed closing off doors, holes, cracks,
to seal off their escape, get rid of them,
in-situ. I didn't want to know how
shrugging, nonchalant above my unrest.
He asked if I'd like to go down there
Nope! Why would I call you, mister?

I don't need to witness, pry anything open.
Please contain, cover, kill,
deal with what's excavated—
exorcise, exterminate, exile, as you will.
So he kept me out of the cleansing, shielding
my emancipation from pesky invaders.
Hours of silence reigned, and peace
Then... *Bloody Hell!* A remnant voice,
squeaking, sending up last calls and pricks.
I sat in fury at the audacity of insignificance!

In days, even that stopped
A final peace! Now I'm really saved
from invasions of a prowling past...
Until a stink began, an odor emanating
from decades gone persisting, demanding
I descend, reexamine the remains,
cremate the cadavers, clear the carcasses,
bury the ashes, or submerge in rivers
Only then walk back up in agony of rebirth
to remake my home, my airs, my voyage.

Finding It—A Pantoum

Sometimes I find myself
listening to words of people
I surmise from my reaction
they're asking for the usual trade

Listening to words of people
I know I can't possibly make it
They're asking for the usual trade
Join the clan in exchange for comfort, collusion

I know I can't possibly make it
sick of the nodding heads of falsehoods who want me
to join the clan in exchange for comfort, collusion
I pose questions that shouldn't be asked

Sick of the nodding heads of falsehoods
I refuse their free bestowing of victimhood
I pose questions that shouldn't be asked!
They frown, then rage at my ingratitude

I refuse their free bestowing of victimhood
for I was taught the prideful sin of self-respect
They frown, then rage at my ingratitude for
they don't know my suffering people who refused to beg

For I was taught the prideful sin of self-respect,
No wallowing in chains, be in freedom where you are
They don't know my suffering people who refused to beg.
Instead, my people melted their chains to build cities.

Vaishali Kulkarni

Vaishali Kulkarni is a qualified Pharma professional working in the medical and healthcare industry for about 20 years. She is from Maharashtra, India and holds immense love for her mother tongue, Marathi. She expresses her love for Marathi through her poetry. Though she covers a variety of topics in her writing, most of her poems engage feelings, relationships, and nature. She has created word and mixed-media art in collaboration with Varsha More under the hash tag *#chitrolivarshalichya* wherein the words by Vaishali and artwork of Varsha intertwine into unique artwork.

नजरा

खोल खोल गाभार्‍यात आत
अशी किती अनंत सत्ये
एक मला ठाउक आणि फक्त
मलाच ठाऊक...
मी टिपल्या कितीक नजरा
लोचट.. अधाशी ..धुर्त जरा...
चोरट्या आणि काही धीट निर्लज्जही..
केल्या बन्द लिफाफ्यात
न बोलता ठेवून दिल्या
खोल खोल आतल्या कप्प्यात...
करीन विसर्जन सगळ्यांच
एक तर माझ्या अंती
नाहीतर त्यांच्या...
सांगीन सगळी गुपितं गंगेला...
वाहू देईन सगळ्यानाच..
आधी माझ्या डोळ्यातून
मग तिच्या प्रवाहात...

आनुवंशिकता

खूप खूप वर्ष आधी..
माझ्या आत एक बी रुजलं

कित्येक शरीरातून उडत उडत
आलेलं माझ्यातच झिरपलं..

हळूहळू त्या बी च रोप
आणि रोपाच झाड झालं..

माझे हात माझे पाय
माझे डोके सर्वांग त्यानं झाकलं

वेदनेची बी तिला वेदनेचीच फळं
वेदनेच झाड माझ्यातच बहरलं

झाडाला सतत जखमांची पानगळ
खपली वर खपली अंगण खपल्यानी भरलं

आत बहर बाहेर बहर
वेदनेच्या खतावर झाड मोठ झालं

वर्षा मागून वर्षे झडली
तगलं तसच,आताशा झाड निष्पर्ण झालं

नवीन खपली धरत नाही जुनी ही फार गळत नाही
वेदना आत मुरलीय आता,दुःख जरा स्थिरावलं

एकच विचार असतो आत
एकच इच्छा.. आपल झालं ते झालं

आपल्यातलं बी उडत उडत
पुढच्या पिढीत न रुजो म्हंजे झालं..

ओळख

किती दिस झाले नाही लिहिले मी काही
कोरी वही कोरी पाने कोरे मन कोरे राही

कोलाहल सभोवती आत झिरपत नाही
देता आवाज स्वतः ला प्रतिसाद सुद्धा नाही

कशी माझीच मलाही ओळखच पटेनाता
कसा कशानेही आता मला फरक पडेना

मी तीच का की जिच्या उरी लाटांचा कहर
शाई होऊन उधाणे पानी मनीचा सागर

ओहोटले माझ्यातले जशी सागरा ओहोटी ,
झरा आटला कोरडा , जशी रेती वाळवंटी

जणू अवसेची रात माझ्या आत उतरली
कसे बोथट मी झाले माझी सर्व धार गेली

वाट पाहते मी आता कधी पहाट होईल
लेखणीला पान्हा नवा कधी पुन्हा उजाडेल

पुन्हा आरसा पाहता पुन्हा दिसावी कविता
व्हावा पुन्हा नवा जन्म जुनी ओळख पटता

अशी यावी ती सकाळ घेऊनिया शुभाक्षरे
सृजनाची उन्हे पुन्हा उजळूदे बंद दारे

अनोळखी

आज आरशातल्या माझ्या डोळ्यात
डोळे घालून बघितले जरा..
नजर रोखून..
एकटक पापणी न लवता..

कुणीतरी अनोळखी परक
रोखून बघतय अस वाटलं ..
हा तोच देह..
सतत गेली काही वर्ष
माझ्या बरोबर राहतोय माझ्यात घुसून

हे तेच नाव..
सतत काही वर्ष कानावर पडतंय
लोक आम्हाला त्या नावाने हाक मारतात
आम्हाला दोघीना
तो देह ,ते नाव पण परकं वाटल अचानक.

शहरा आल्यासारखं झालं..
कळेना कुणावर माझ्यावर किं तीच्यावर
चालमेल झाली क्षणभर

कुणी तरी हलवलं आणि भानावर आले
क्षणभरासाठी विलग झालेलं अनोळखी काही
पुन्हा बिलगलं..पुन्हा ओळखीचं झालं..

जीवात जीव आला आणि आम्ही दोघी
आरसा सोडून मार्गस्थ झालो

कोलाहल

आताशा मन शांततेच्या शोधात असतं..
पूर्वी रमायच गलक्यात आता तस नसतं

आता ना आत्मस्तुतीचे पोवाडे गावे वाटत
ना त्यावर लाळघोट्या टाळ्यांचा गजर आवडत

मला नकोय आता कुणाचीच ललकारी
नको आता कुठल्याच विजयाची तुतारी

बास झाले रे खोटे नाटे आता जयजयकार
त्रास होतोय, कुजबुजीत ऐकू येतो विखार

ऐकायचीत मला आता माझीच स्पंदने
श्वासाची लय आणि धमन्यातली आंदोलने

दुनियेच्या गोंगाटात वय भाजल सारं
एकच इच्छा आता हा उतरावा ज्वर

शांत होऊन आता जरा बाह्य कोलाहल
ऐकू यावे अंतरातले चांदणे शीतल

नन्हापन

मुझे पेडोंपे पत्ता बनके पत्तोंमे बस जाना है
हरा रंग, हरा बन हरियाली मे घुल जाना है

मुझे किरन सूनहरी पीके खुद सोना बन जाना है
दीन मे पिली धूप तो रात अंधियारा बन छाना है

मुझे चंदापास जो तारा है उसको जाके छूना है
और बर्फ की छोटी बुंदे बन हिमालय भी होना है

मुझे गंगा बन,गंगा संग, गंगा मे बह जाना हैं
फुलोंकी खुशबू पाके हवाओ पर लहराना है

मुझे तितली नन्ही उसके नन्हे पंखो उपर सोना है
अपने "आप" को पिघलाके बस इतना नन्हा होना है

तेरी याद

तेरी याद जब आती है मन गिला गिला होता है
जुलै की बारिश जैसे आंख से आंसू बहते है

गुस्सा भी आ जाता है कर याद जो तूंने बोला था
अब प्यार नहीं है तुझसे मुझे ये बोलके मुझको टाला था

एक बार नही कयी बार हुआ तू रुठा मैने मनाया था
हम दोनो का खस्ता रिश्ता ना टूटे मैने संभाला था

अब फिर तू मुझसे रूठा है तेरी रूठ ने की आदत है
पर मैं दुविधा मे हु अबके फिर जोड़ू या अब तोडना है

ये जानता है दिमाग मेरा अब कूछ न बचा, सब झूठा है
पर मन अब भी है मान रहा तू दीलसे मुझको चाहता है

दिल दिमाग की होड मे अबके दिमाग ने बाजी जिती है
जा अपने मन की कर ले तू , मुझसे रीहा तुझे कर दिया है

तू लौट के शायद आयेगा गर तू सचमुच मे मेरा है
गर ना भी आया गीला नहीं तेरी यादो मे बस जीना है

Lalit Kumar

Lalit Kumar writes a regular column in *India Currents Magazine* sharing his passion for adventure and travel. He is the author of two poetry books, **Yosemite of my Heart** and **Years Spent**. He has also been published in various Anthologies including poems in California's poet laureate's anthology.

LalitKumarOnline.Com

The Joshua Tree of Mojave

Dry, arid, desert landscape of Mojave
spartan-like, feisty under the relentless sun,
austere rock outcrops, shrubs,
wildflowers under the clear blue sky,
bloom vividly upon a thousand stars in the cover of the night.
A solid trunk of a tree, a poetry
unfurls its branches in a twisted scape
gazing straight upon the starry night,
in deep contemplation of its sparse existence.
Eking out a living of its own,
resilient,
the root seeks water through the fault lines of the desert.
Standing alone in sublime beauty of its harsh climes,
radiating joy to the lone hiker.
In the beauty of a silhouette, it emerges
the Joshua tree of Mojave.

Alone in San Francisco

Sauntering down the Embarcadero
Along the edges of pier 39,
A foggy morning clings to the city,
Rumbling itself awake from slumber.

I trudge along the wooden pier,
The waves lap at the jetty
The winds howl in my ears
A pelican nonchalantly flaps its wings
And flies past my view ahead.

It's not so lonely, after all
The nature is resplendent in its spread today,
The winds, the waves, the ocean
Seem to have no bearing
To the seasons of my mind.
Nature is constant,
My mind shifts with each seed of thought.

I am not so lonely, after all
I open my arms
To welcome the oncoming wind
feeling it directly on my face.
I let it caress
My skin and my face
I feel it ruffle my hair,
And I close my eyes to
Witness the love of my friend.

I jump in the oncoming waves
The blues of Pacific
Is as cold, as the thaw in my heart.
It's an instant commingling
Of two long lost lovers
For whom the distance has not dimmed
The light of their hearts.

Distant memory has a way of its own
To ebb and flow with the tide.
A dream can rise aflutter with the waves
Or sink to the bottom
With the changing tides, and time.

The ocean water
I feared it may drown me,
Instead it taught me,
how to swim with the tide.

The Places We Inhabit—A Pantoum

There is something in the air of California,
I have spent my thirties belonging here.
My parents have grown old in another land,
what was it about California that made me stay?

I have spent my thirties living here,
nurturing my sense of adventure in Tahoe, Monterey
    and the places around,
What was it about California that made me stay?
I thought I had found my answer when I chose to build a home.

I nurtured my sense of adventure in Tahoe, Monterey
    and the places around,
yet my body is full of longing for the distant land.
I thought I had found my answer when I chose to build a home,
to my disbelief, the passing years added up
    too soon, fifteen to be exact.

My body is full of longing for the distant land,
who thought that my parents would grow old?
The passing years added up too soon, fifteen to be exact.
I inhabited two worlds together, one in the body
    and the other in the mind.

Who thought that my parents would grow old?
I remember what my mother told me before I left.
All these years, I inhabited two worlds together,
    one in the body and the other in the mind,
The body accreted layers of memory from California, the mind
    remained fossilized since fifteen years from the distant land.

I remember what my mother told me before I left,
there is something in the air of California.
The body accreted layers of memory from California,
    the mind remained fossilized
    since fifteen years from the distant land,
My parents have grown old in another land.

Fear or Fire

There is a tiny spark
Smoldering just beneath my fear.
Raring its little head
whenever I want to leap.

Niggling fear or the Raging fire
whom should I choose?
I choose fear,
feels my life beginning to shrink.

I choose the raging fire
I expand beyond my proportion.
Something inside of me
begins to take a shape.
That smoke from the smoldering fire
begins to clear,
as I leap,
beyond my courage.

Elham Malik

Elham Malik, a poet, educator, and engineer, recently graduated with a Ph.D., studying the human spirit in systems and the silences in structure. Her poems map the unseen currents beneath roles, routines, and relationships—where the self listens, questions, and is changed. Emergent from contemplative traditions and the immediacy of everyday encounters, her poems disclose the unseen harmonies linking lives, a subtle revolt against fragmentation through the language of wholeness.

With Nilkantha, In the Grace of the Undying Flame

Side by side with you, O Blue-throated Flame,
I walk, not in pride, but recalling Your name.
Every step with awareness, every breath a quiet prayer,
And you're Dawn, and in your light, I mend.

You who had the world's dark brew in Your throat,
And bear its burden with not a word to gloat—
And let whatever you take fall with you.
To serve in dignity, and persevere through it all.

I desire no titles inscribed upon a monument.
Only a heart that is truly yours.
whether in happiness or sorrow's pain,
May stillness ground me in all things.

O Mahayogi, staff in hand, sitting
Learn not to dominate, but to listen.
To tread through the fire with a silent determination
To be no one, and be full.

I, like the Nilkantha bird,
Travel through the world, unseen and unheeded—
Blue flash in the bend of shadow
Ethereal beauty, a loyal companion.

Let my hands be soothing, my eyes be light,
Refuge for spirits in the quiet of the evening.
To not rise above, but to be close by—
With the broken, with the brave, fearless.

May I become like ashes upon Your brow,
Charred by ego, but radiant today.
Let my bones resonate with Your cosmic dance,
Where time disappears, and hearts move forward.

And when I fall, as mere mortals fall,
May I rise to lean into You—
Your name in every breath I breathe
In life, a protection, in death, a wake.

No throne I beseech, no seat with flowers—
To reflect Your sweet mercy alone.
Make me a vessel, open and broad,
Let others drink, and be content.

And here I stand, true and steadfast—
No crown, no entitlement—only walking with You.
One step, one breath, through day and night
Always aligned, always in sight.

Kālo'smi: The Yoga of Becoming

Not silence as surrender,
but the radiance of presence.
A quiet strength, refined by devotion—
the soul, unwavering,
braided into breath, bone, and being,
not as a burden, but as consecrated flame.

This is not endurance for its own sake,
but a sacred offering,
tempered through time
within the temple of the body.

God does not delay in cruelty—
there is no malice in the stillness.
Only a hallowed preparation.
What seems withheld is often grace in waiting.

In wholehearted, deliberate motion,
unmoored from reward,
there is a union—
a stillness that moves without grasping.

Worthiness is not a prize,
but a quiet unveiling,
emerging not at the end,
but unfolding along the way.

Sorrow did not come to break,
but to reveal—
to peel back the illusions
we outgrew in silence.

Each grief: a scripture in ash,
a flame that burns falsehoods away.
It speaks not in ruin,
but in raw remembrance.

Pleasure and pain—twin tutors—
drawing the spirit inward,
away from grasping desire,
toward the stillness at the center.

They whispered: Be still—
in joy, in ache—
for both are passing tides,
waves returning to silence.

Release the harvest.
Let the fruit ripen without striving.
Let it fall, if it must—
and offer it back without resistance.

When the season calls it home,
let there be no clinging.
For all ripeness has its rhythm,
and release is part of ripening.

Confusion once knelt,
buckling beneath choice.
The bow slipped—not from weakness,
but from trembling at the edge of knowing.

Then came the whisper:
This is a sacred war.
You are not the doer—
you are the fire, not the flicker.

The furnace—not the flame.
The stillness within the strike.
The force beneath the form.
The pulse that does not falter.

Solitude returned like a forest season—
not retreat, but homecoming—
a return to the hush
beneath all sound.

What seemed like void
was silent blooming.
Memory faded—
but the body remembered the hymn.

Even in stillness, life stirred:
breath threaded through marrow,
cells sang their quiet labor,
and time continued its weaving.

There is a name for the watcher,
but no form can hold it.
No tale can contain it—
only silence can witness.

The true self—unborn, undying—
moves not, but sees.
It remains as storms rise,
as worlds break and pass away.

What is real
cannot be unmade.
It stands beneath the falling,
the breaking, the fading.

Each fall: a lesson.
Each unmet longing, a summons—
to release without closing,
to surrender and remain open.

With every returning storm,
wisdom distills in silence—
unmoved by chaos,
unbound by mere knowledge.

Then, action rises—
not for applause,
nor out of fear,
but as the tide of clear intent.

To move as the hour asks,
to serve without possession,
to become the very doing—
this is freedom.

There is mastery in letting go,
and liberation in the gift.
The lotus does not bloom by command—
it waits for warmth, for light, for timing.

Then it opens—without struggle.
So too, the soul unfolds.
Not in rebellion against time,
but in rhythm with its truth.

What once seemed barren
was never void—
but a quiet gathering of force,
a sanctuary of gestation.

An unbroken stillness,
where transformation took root.
Waiting was not absence,
but becoming in slow breath.

Breath ripened into resolve.
Presence formed into shape.
And so, the ascent began—
not ahead of time,

But as Time itself.
"I am Time," says the voice—
and in that moment,
the journey is complete.

The Resilient Thread of Life

Life starts not at birth, but where it turns,
At every sudden bend where comfort stops.
In the quiet interval between what was and is,
We discover the soul's chrysalis.

Transitions emerge from muted pain,
In each fall, the ground we break
Empowers seeds of strength we never knew—
An unseen path, but a path true.

Change is the loom, and struggle the thread,
Bitter and sweet, spread tightly.
Tears, as dew, upon petals lie,
Instructing hearts that they love them best.

Blessed are we, as we walk this path.
To rise and fall and grow each day.
Human existence—a sacred opportunity
To shed illusion, dance the dance.

The same designs recur in fresh form.
Revisiting wounds we thought were lies.
And pass from us like a dream,
Nothing is lost in impermanence.

Relationships break, repair, and blur,
Ego, time the artist, memory the stir.
Yet in this fleeting, quivering tide,
The self itself has to be the guide.

Let the weave be loose or tight,
Every knot a lesson, every tear a light.
Only after adopting this earthly form
Soul can rise, and spirit can ascend.

Strive not to possess, but to embody—
The thread, the seam, the divine tapestry, the One.

Beyond the Mirage of Binary Veil

In the temple's twilight stands Ardhanarishwar,
half woman, half man, merged in cosmic dance.
One draped in silk and the other in tiger-skin;
one hand gives a lotus, the other raises a trident.
Two eyes share a common vision under a single third eye,
and two halves that beat together in harmony.
The Father and Mother of the universe combined in one person,
the womb and seed of creation inseparable.
The god speaks in silence—apparently divided, yet one.

Vishnu, the Preserver, even adopted the form of Mohini,
an enchantress with nectar of immortality on her lips.
Gods and demons stood in awe, mesmerized by her divine beauty,
not realizing that the bright maiden was Vishnu disguised.
In that sacred form, the god was transformed
　　into a goddess but not diminished,
demonstrating that the soul is able to adopt a thousand faces
and never violate its unity.
A divine masquerade, not deception—
a truth wearing form like light through mist.

In silent houses, under the same moon,
he cries into his pillow so that no one may witness his sadness.
Somewhere else, a woman lets out the tear she suppressed all day.
Theirs is a taste as salty, as weighty a pain as
though they each believe they weep alone.
Sorrow is not masculine or feminine—it calls upon
　　every heart alike.
And joy also bursts forth with similar light.

The giggles of a girl and the guffaws of a boy
arise from the same delight, unpartitioned and pure;
varied voices—high and low—singing a boundless song together.

He was instructed to be unrelenting, to put on
    armor and conceal his sorrow;
she was taught to be kind, to swallow her flaming temper and smile.
Steel and silk—he hardened his heart, she silenced her lips—
costumes culturally tailored to cover up who they really are.
But midnight is aware that his citadel of stoicism fissures,
and her tranquility hides a raging strength.
In his heart is a gentleness that longs to be expressed;
there is a ferocity waiting to be seen within her.
Each harbors the other's secret, a reflection of the other's potential.
Two actors on society's stage, reciting their lines—
yet in the wings, their true selves whisper in unison.

Submerged underneath epidermis and narrative, hidden
    from 'woman' and 'man', is the soul.
The soul is not male or female—like fire, like wind, it just is.
It burns with freedom and boundlessness, invisible and unconfined.
In each of us lives that ancient light beneath the labels 'he' and 'she'.
Like a white ray through the prism of life,
our single pure light is divided into hues
    known as 'male' and 'female'.
But take away the prism and the light is whole again.
Just as evening brings together day and night in a single sky,
our dualities dissolve into truth as illusion recedes.
We are rays from one sun, leaves of one tree, waves of one sea.
One among many, many in one: this is the soul's secret song.
We were never two; we have always been one.

Beneath Maya's Veil: The Hidden Self in Every Disguise

In the dream of Maya, we wander—each soul
    a solitary actor on the stage of life,
mistaking the mask it wears for its true face.
The One Self, refracted through illusion,
    splinters into countless selves,
like a single moon reflected in a hundred ponds.
We chase those scattered lights and forget
    the sky from which they shine.
Yet a silent thread of consciousness stitches every heart together—
each life drawing from the same invisible ocean of Being.

The king's laughter and the beggar's tear ripple
    through that same sea;
we are waves from a single source—when one rises
    or falls, all feel the pull.
In the city of mirrors, affluence and destitution
    gaze past one another.
Glass towers cast shadows over rusted shanties.
While banquet halls gleam in the heights,
a child rummages through refuse in the alley below.

Heaven and hell share the same street,
separated only by the illusions we uphold.
Blinded by greed, we desecrate the very earth that cradles us.
Rivers once sacred now run black with industry's waste.
Forests fall silent, their trees sacrificed for concrete and gold.
Smokestacks rise like false gods,
as we forget the sacredness of breath, soil, and sky.

But poison knows no caste, no class.
Avarice returns upon all,
and its weight is heaviest upon the voiceless.
The barefoot child coughs on another's luxury.
The fading eyes of a tiger in a dying forest
    reflect our insatiable hunger.
The silent earth bears it all—
her grief carried in erratic winds and untimely rains.

Those who never tasted from the feast bear the burden of its excess.
Their cries are drowned in the machinery of progress.
How long will this sorrowful wheel turn,
dragging us through darkness life after life?

Must we endlessly reenact this tale of separation,
age after age, incarnation after incarnation?

Or will we remember the ancient truth—tat tvam asi,
"Thou art That"—
and see the One gazing out from every pair of eyes?

Will the morning ever dawn
when all rivers—lost and longing—find their way back to the sea?

Prerona Mukerjee

I have loved telling stories since I was a little child. While stories spill out of my mind incessantly, only a few find their way into written words. My poems are thoughts, dreams, and feelings captured in words; confessions and confidences I cannot make. I was born in Aleppo, Syria; I grew up in Calcutta, India; I spent my youth in Edinburgh, United Kingdom. Like the wild parrots and the sea lions, somehow I found my way to San Francisco, and there I stayed. My poems are about the loss of home, the longings of the exiled, and the tax of the road.

Love Notes

I touch your cheek as you sleep
Soft and furry like the peaches you love.
I eavesdrop on your secret sleepy mumblings,
I steal a kiss, and steel myself to slip away.

Are you avoiding me, she asks,
As I rush away from the mirror?
Why do you get so busy,
whenever I reach out for you?

I cling to the little pearls of sisterhood.
I collect charms for my bracelet.
We rush, we pause, we rush again.
Busy as hives, buzzing side by side.

At night I collapse by you, speechless
The day finally done,
This fallow vessel we share,
Ours alone, this silent moonrise.

The photo on the wall could be a mirror. I smile.
Was I really that small, snuggled up against you?
How deliciously the world would fall away
How peacefully I wrapped myself in you; and I rested.

Oh Calcutta!

Like a corpse suddenly quivers,
When she hears her beloved's name,
My broken heart reanimates for a moment,
When I hear her say those words:
Where in Calcutta do you live, I'd asked
Southern Avenue, she'd said.

That night with a clap of pigeons wings,
I find myself again on those streets,
Those old familiar houses, blinking sleepily,
The street dogs stretching lazy limbs, open half an eye,
They smell me, they know me, Or am I still me?
Or an afterbirth, Washing by the gutter, in the dirty rain water.

I waft in the air of that city,
Lost in time,
I waft in the smoke
from the istriwallas bucket of glowing coals
I echo in the screech of the alley cat,
Angry and resentful possessive of the night.
I linger in the sound of someone gargling,
In the water from the street taps gurgling.

I stalk about, with the conference of crows,
My body, my limbs, my stomach, my heart
A patchwork of red rexine rickshaw seats,
Of sprawled blue and white check lungi's,
The underbush of this towering metropolis,
Reclaiming their breath, in sleep, almost human.

Do you remember me? You haunt me.
Tell me once more your forgotten stories.
I was eating your voice, your skin, trying to crawl back into yo—
I was leaving a thread to return to the world.
Light the path that echoes behind me, Give me
    a clue, to the riddle ahead.
I am frozen, a pillar of salt.

Meet me at dawn once more, my cry rings out from the lakes,
The rickshaw wheels spin, to oblivion,
The dramatic tapestry of human generations…
Then a hush of rain washes us traces away.
My chaos, my Calcutta, my name,
My soul's home, forever.

The 6th of August, 2025, San Francisco

You had left me, on a Sunday in Fall.
I was alone with my grief.
I took it for a walk to South Gyle.
We walked for hours.
There was no sidewalk,
But I barely noticed.
The world, a flash speeding by.
I must have seemed drunk; I was.
We went to the mall,
My grief and I;
I bought it a set of salt and pepper shakers; Apropos of nothing.
Haunted by your last words,
by the last look in your eyes,
by knowing I deserted you, Ma.

You left. It is Fall.
And it is twenty years today.
My grief is a secret garden
Bluebells & Anemones bow heads in guilt.
Hand wringing, the geraniums atone their folly,
Proud marigolds and Narcicuss, withered.
Primroses sigh, how do I live without you?
For years have I nurtured
my illicit pain with my guilt
Till it has blossomed a thousand blooms
Haunted by a doubt: Did I deserve your devotion?
Did I deserve your inherited dreams,
Your bid to be free?
I was not brave enough, Ma.

I will always remember that day in Fall.
Look, I'm grown! No more your bright, helpless little bird ...
I've collected a map of furrows, age spots and scars.
Rusty joints, creaking soul, and fractured heart.
I remember your freckles: Like a sky full of stars ...
Bright sienna on your skin like blue veined marble.
We all took turns to trace you with our greedy love.
We only saw your startling smiles,
But how quietly majestic you grieved!
How haunting your eyes, lost in the distance,
How you sometimes sighed; I didn't see.
So many secrets I never asked you,
Many things you told me, unheeded.
I thought you began with me, Ma, I never dared to think of the end.

And now I know, you must have missed me,
How lonely you must have sat, on that rocking chair
Centrestage, silently proud, in that empty house,
you had ruled so long, but now all the citizens had moved on.
Left was you, your notebooks, your bookshelf, your poetry,
The marble busts, porcelain dolls, the statue of the lizard
With the cockroach in its mouth - from the local fair.
You must have waited for the bell to ring.
I was seven when you said one night,
It would be time for you to go, someday.
You said you would come back for me - maybe a ghost
Terrified of the supernatural, I said please don't!
You cried. I didn't understand why.
But you haunt me, anyway, Ma, you dissolved in the air.

Sunday Afternoons, In A Place
That Used To Be Called Calcutta

On Sundays, my grandmother made potatoes with Luchi;
Small, round pieces of bread made of white flour
With thin, soft, and stretchy layers like
the layers of ancient cotton she wrapped herself in
Tender curtains that billowed around her body
A playground, a shelter, a toy ...
My mother and her sister would help her cook sometimes.
They would gather in the grey cement kitchen
And the hushed, urgent buzz of their gossip would escape
On those days I would be shut out of kitchen,
Where usually, I would play on the floor as she cooked.
On those days, I would play on the red mosaic
        floor of the dining room
My ears would hover at the doorway to the kitchen
To steal morsels of stories that may escape.
Some days I would play under the big marble dining table
Its black legs and grayish white underbelly, a familiar canopy
Almost as well known as a second mother.
Then they would all emerge from the kitchen together
They would be transformed into their more public selves
Their dining room selves;
Their little secrets would have been consumed.
And their kitchen selves would have been
tidied away neatly with the nigella seeds, and tumeric.
We would sit and eat together at the table
and they would talk to me In cheerful child voices,
and laugh at my stories again.
Now I am a mother and
I understand the coven,
the brunt of caring,
of brewing a family.

Dreams and Mornings

The peacefully sleeping window
was smashed by a furious sound
a sudden storm in a quiet night
the rain rushed down and stayed
pat pat pat softly soothing
the night went back to sleep
I lost my way
in a maze of humans
playing, laughing, living out loud.
i was circum-navigating a joyride
an old friend came and kissed me
a lost face returned by a dream
Suddenly it is morning. Climax interrupted
Jump out of bed. Brush. Change.
Hurry! Hurry! We're late! We're late!
Let's Go! Eat! I love you!
Remember to be brave! Be a good boy!
And don't forget to eat your lunch! Be safe, be safe, be safe ...

The Fairy Garden in my Backyard

My shoulder has started to nag me again
The gnawing knuckles, a surly spouse.

There is a Chickadee hopping about the bird pond
in the backyard. He is so determined to be clean!

Did I shut my eyes when the blows fell?
I can't remember - I sold my memories for peace.

The bird cocks his black and white head to look at me
Querying my intent. Where am I going with this, indeed?

My scars are fading now; like a friend
    who was knocking on my door,
Saying, Come! cry with me, but is beginning to tire and turn away.

The waterfall in the backyard was made by the previous owner
A love story we inherited, a poem for his wife, who loved birds.

I block the whining ache, the wisps of memory,
    and focus on the dishes.
The sink stares brightly out of a window, at the backyard.

Water whispers over rocks. Their daughter
    had collected the stones, I'd heard
Refuse rebuilt with so much love, up-cycling before it was a fashion.

I do not have the courage, the strength, to mourn. I freeze. I run.
I watch my blood pool and wait for my silent cries to congeal.

The bird plays in the water, unaware;
The lilies tower over her like an enchanted jungle.

Please don't fade, scar. I did not own you yet, but I will try.
You are my prize, my proof, that I too once felt.

The birds, raccoons, neighbors' cats: my backyard
    is a watering hole.
None of them know that we have claimed this land
    exclusively for our own.

Nature is not always gentle and sweet; romantic …
Nature is also the tiger swatting dead an ant. Also you and I …

A giant eucalyptus tree towers over our fairy garden.
    It is the neighbors.
I stare at it spell bound, whenever there is a storm.
    What would it crush, if it falls?

The eucalyptus came from a foreign land, whether or not
    by willing consent, but
With the native trees growing nearby, it has weathered
    many storms side by side.

When I was first banished here, I made friends
    with the Pelicans. And now
this Eucalyptus, is the friend of my silence, witness
    of my solitary nights.

Time

I thought time would leave my essence unchanged,
Life would crumple my skin,
And ravage my face.

I thought time would not leak to my soul
And I would remain,
my essence, my "I-ness" un-corrupted.

Till I got wrinkles on my tongue,
I thought age was just a number.
Then I understood: age is wrinkles on the tongue.

Sullen, reluctant body,
Rebel eyes and vanishing eyebrows that,
I can't raise with quite the same effect.

My body, once my unquestioned dominion,
Is feathered by rumbles of rebellion.
Nothing of note has happened yet, but I fear, what next?

They say you're as old as you feel: my heart
    is exhausted from feeling.
They say you're as young as your soul: my soul is as fresh as a child's.
I have wrinkles on my tongue, and my feet tap restlessly.

Making You

How did you make me, Mummy; you love to ask.
I smile quietly. By dissolving my Self, I want to say
Sleepless nights
Hands let go
Friends abandoned
A mother disobeyed
Lover neglected
Love redefined
Patience built like a bulging muscle
Work abandoned, dreams relinquished
Many many commitments betrayed,
Head hung in shame
Life, abandoned
My days, my breath shortened
To your weight in my arms
My universe shrunk to the light in your eyes
My dreams shredded to make a quilt
My tiring breath, floating beneath your questions
My steps measured, to be your guide
My whole being, wrapped around you keep you warm, dry, safe
as long as you need, Then permission to be discarded
With a smile and a blessing
My good memories burnt like driftwood
     to make a fire that will warm you
My bad memories spur me on: I don't want you to have any;
The impotent hubris of parent-hood.
The entitlement and safety with which you use me,
Wiping your grubby tiny hands on my me-hood,
Using me, effacing me, grinding me down to fodder ...
My body, my strength, my memories, my stories, my labour,
The dinner I cooked for hours, recruited imperiously,
To feed your dreams, your games, your flight ...
That is how I made you, my love.

This Body

This body broken by childbirth
This brain fogged from years of sleeplessness
This heart sore from loving
These tired arms, a dear blankie, this tummy a pillow
These clothes marked with dinner, little hands wiped
These knees sore from squatting to kiss each hurtee
Mummy is not a hanky, not a trash can, not a chair
You giggle. This security this entitlement, This deed of entitlement,
This body I sold to buy for you.
       As those who came and went before me
These essays in living, dreams and tattered stories
I pass on to you
This body, I burned To make yours
This life that I inherited, I give you
These dreams they gave me, are yours.

Yogesh Patel

Yogesh Patel received an MBE for literature in 2020. With many books, film, radio play, and LP records, Patel's poems appear on the **Poetry Wall** of the **Royal Society of Literature** and featured at Cambridge University's Language Library. He runs *Skylark Publications UK*. Extensively published, an award-winning poet, he has also received the **Freedom of the City of London.**

Tandava

I never promised anything. The walls
stood patient, mute. They felt what struck, then stayed.
They tasted breathless blows, and through it all,
they watched the dust rehearse its slow cascade.

The ruins wonder how the *home* withdrew —
its pulse dissolved, but structures still remain.
Omelettes cracked; the fungi crept right through.
The toast reached for its butter, all in vain.

Since then, each morning grinds beneath our teeth.
The bricks still chew what we pretend to clear.
I name absurdities — *"Jazzy sunnies!"* — brief
bright offerings to keep the fiction near.

And yet, I know: when you appear,
the Sun folds back. The shadows dance. They hear.

www.ingramcontent.com/pod-product-compliance
Lightning Source LLC
Chambersburg PA
CBHW030529130626
46549CB00007B/3168